A Pilgrim's Guide

Oberammergau
and its Passion Play

By David Houseley & Raymond Goodburn

A Pilgrims Guide

Contents

Acknowledgements

The Authors would like to thank the many people who have helped consider-
ably to make this book possible. In particular, Hannes Hiergeist of the local
Tourist Office in Oberammergau; Harald Rettelbach Press Officer to the
Passion Play Committee, and Otto Huber, Deputy Director of the Passion
Play. Pictures from the 1990 Passion Play by Thomas Klinger are reproduced
by permission of the Gemeinde Oberammmergau, as also are some pictures
of the Village and surroundings. Others are from the German National Tourist
Office and the Tourist Office in Oberammmergau.
  They are also indebted to Ingrid Shafer, Professor of Philosophy, Religion and
Interdisciplinary Studies at the University of Science and Arts of Oklahoma, for
the provision of the Synopsis of the Play.

Facing Page: *Inside the Parish Church*

Preface

This book is designed for those many thousands of English speaking people who will travel to a lovely corner of Bavaria to experience the most famous Passion Play in the world. It is performed in the most delightful surroundings by a cast of local amateurs who, through their own faith and passion will transmit the story of Jesus' trials, suffering and resurrection in a manner which can only affect the hearts of all the thousands present at each performance, even though many of them will not be able to understand a word of what is being spoken on stage. Of course, the story and the message are well known, but the manner of its telling is without doubt unique, and an experience, which will not be forgotten. The authors hope that the book will assist in preparation for the visit, be helpful whilst there, and that it will also become a valued souvenir, helping to revive many happy memories.

For the majority of visitors, their stay in Oberammergau will be all too brief, so that it is all the more important to obtain the maximum benefit from their time there. For that reason we have not set out to provide a hugely detailed history, nor an extensive tour of the area. Our aim is to enable the reader to understand the Play and follow its action; to be aware of the traditions and background against which it is performed; and to understand why it evokes such strength of feeling. We hope it will also show what a wealth of attraction, beauty and interest is to be found both in the village itself and in the surrounding area.

If we succeed in these objectives and also in encouraging the first time visitor to Oberammergau to return to the area another year for a longer and more leisurely stay, we shall be well satisfied.

David Houseley
Raymond Goodburn

Facing Page: *View towards the Kofel*

Welcome to Oberammergau
From Otto Huber, Second Director of the Passion Play

On behalf of the Community of Oberammergau and the Passion Play Committee, I extend a warm welcome to all our English-speaking visitors, to the Passion Play 2000. You make up almost half of all those who will see the play. After all, this play is directed not only at the German-speaking audience, but to all of humanity.

For the year 2000,the village of Oberammergau gave Christian Stückl the task of preparing a new production and to me the task to re-writing the script, based oh the text by Pater Othmar Weis and Fr Daisenberger. The most essential goal of the play is a living and compelling proclamation of the Christian faith to the contemporary visitor in the light of current Biblical scholarship and the recommendations of the Second Vatican Council that "one may not portray the Jews as discarded by God or rejected by God or cursed as though this conclusion could be drawn on the basis of Holy Scripture".

It is important to emphasise that Jesus was born and died an observant Jew, that He was executed by collusion of an envious Jewish religious faction and a brutal, ambitious Roman governor, and that, tragically ,for many centuries, the gospel message was perverted and passion plays became the occasion of murderous attacks by Christians on Jews. We also know that the genre of Passion Play was one of the contributing factors to the rise of 20th century anti-semitism that spawned the Holocaust. In fact, shortly before he died, Pope John XXIII asked that the Lord forgive Christians for having cursed the Jews and having crucified Him a second time in their flesh. We did our best to have this production reflect these concerns while maintaining as much of the traditional play as possible. In these efforts we were supported by a large number of highly respected Christian and Jewish scholars.

Professor Mödl, the official Catholic advisor for Oberammergau, appointed by Cardinal Wetter, praised the new text: "Wherever people are selfish or malicious, they behave as human beings who just happen to be Jewish. The evil characters as well as the virtuous ones are primarily human beings and only secondarily Jews. In order to emphasise this, a new group was introduced into the Passion Play, members of the High Council who demand a fair trial for Jesus. In this way, the dangerous all-inclusive reproach that the evil Jews had crucified Jesus has been eliminated."

In no way can the guilt for the death of Jesus be contained in any kind of national or ethnic category, for finally, the ruthless might with which Jesus was crushed by a Roman executioner is no other than the ruthless might which crushed an inmate of a concentration camp.

This Introduction does not offer space for a detailed discussion of all the changes. Hence, listing a few of the most essential revisions must suffice.

Anti-Jewish stereotypes of money-hungry merchants have been cut, along with an entire story line, the intrigue of the merchants driven by Jesus out of the Temple. In addition, in the new text, Judas is shown as motivated not by greed but ideology. As a Zealot, he wants to overthrow the Romans and expects Jesus to use his power to lead the People Israel to victory. When Jesus insists that his kingdom is not of this world, Judas speculates that he can provoke his master and friend to demonstrate his messianic might if he finds himself in a truly perilous situation. When previously in diverse chorus scenes and other musically formulated texts, Judas the betrayer was attacked with curses and invectives, now, in keeping with the statement of Jesus, "Judge not so you will not be judged," such denunciations are eliminated. A large portion of the dialogue involving Pilate was newly written to show him as unscrupulous leader of the occupation forces, no more attractive than his appointee, the Sadducee Caiphas, who places himself above God whom he is supposed to serve, and deals with Jesus as though he and his Council were the highest authority respected by all the various Jewish factions of the age. It is important to emphasise that precisely because the Passion Play is based on the gospel, it is not a historic docudrama, but a play of faith.

All the old prologues were re-written. We eliminated potentially offensive living tableaux and added a series of new living tableaux. We focussed on the fact that the subjects of the tableaux should both represent important central moments of Jewish faith history and portray Jesus in the tradition of the Prophets who called human beings away from their false gods in order to lead them toward the living God who spoke to Moses out of the thorn bush. I hope with all my heart that we will succeed in transforming the images originating in Hebrew scripture from their former status as stumbling blocks into building material for bridges between Christians and their Jewish brothers and sisters.

In this sense, I consider the Oberammergau Passion Play 2000 a unique opportunity, especially appropriate at the cusp of the new millennium, for introducing Jesus as Jew among Jews, and to help heal the tragic rupture that has separated the children of Abraham for far too long.

Otto Huber

The Oberammergau Story

The Passion Play has its roots in the medieval mystery plays, which were common all over Europe in the Middle Ages. They existed in several countries, including Britain, where the plays at Chester and Coventry are still performed. Plays which told the story of the Passion of Christ were a later development, but they also continue in places other than Oberammergau, particularly in Austria where the best known are at Erl and Thiersee. They can be traced back in many places as far as the 13th century and were often given as part of the Easter celebrations, but very little is known of their development until the year 1632, when the plague or 'black death' was sweeping through Europe.

The continent was by then some ten years into the 'Thirty Years War' and a year earlier, in 1631, the Protestant army of the Swedish King Gustavus Adolphus had heavily defeated the Catholics at Breitenfeld, and went on to take Wurzburg and Munich. The whole of Bavaria was being ravaged by gangs of marauding soldiers who, being unpaid and underfed, went on orgies of rape and pillage wherever they could, thus helping to spread the disease, which claimed more than a million lives throughout Saxony and Bavaria alone.

The small village of Oberammergau had managed to keep the plague at bay, mainly because of its geographical position, surrounded by mountains and accessible only in the summer months. The nearby village of Ettal with its Monastery, was attacked, but the villagers of Oberammergau, by keeping a constant vigil and controlling the movements of strangers, were able to stay free of the disease. Until, that is, a villager who had been living away, was overcome by homesickness, plus a desire to attend the anniversary celebrations in his home village, stole back under cover of darkness, unknowingly bringing the plague to his own people.

Within months, some 84 inhabitants had died. The whole village met in the church and prayed fervently for deliverance. The members of the Church Council made a solemn vow before the altar that they would perform, every tenth year, a Play of the Saviour's bitter suffering and death, if God would deliver them from the disease. From that day, it is recorded, there were no more deaths.

It was common enough, in the 17th century, to attribute any form of disaster to the Hand of God, and to believe that such pestilence was sent as a punishment. Consequently, it was thought, some form of penitence and expression of faith taken in a collective and public way, might avert the further wrath

Facing Page: *The Betryal of Jesus (1990 play)*

of the Almighty. Hence the vow taken by the villagers in July of 1633.

The performance of a Passion Play in fulfilment of a vow is not unique, but in Oberammergau it has a remarkable record of survival and continuity, despite wars, military occupations, and even an anti-religious edict during a period of secularisation. It is this persistence which has given the Oberammergau play its prominence amongst all other such productions and its renown throughout the Christian world. The first performance was in 1634 and it was repeated every ten years until 1674, when it was decided to bring the performance to the beginning of each decade. So it was performed again in 1680 and continued in this way until 1770, when it was banned by a decree of the Prince-Elector of Bavaria. It was twice reprieved, and at other times held under conditions of great secrecy, but in spite of world wars and other difficulties is has remained almost in unbroken sequence ever since.

Originally, there was just one performance, at Easter. But by 1880 it is recorded that the disturbed times allowed for only five performances, which were not enough to satisfy the demands of all those who wanted to witness the fulfilment of the vow, and three more were arranged for the following year. By 1840 the Play had become internationally known and had begun to attract pilgrims from other lands. By 1869 there were 21 performances and the future King Edward VII of England was one of those who saw the 1870 Play. By 1900 the number of performances had risen to 46, and in the present era there are usually some 90 performances which are seen by about half a million people.

Although the Play is still normally performed in the first year of each decade, there have been some exceptions. The 1920 series was postponed by two years because of the devastation caused by World War I, and a special series was put on in 1934 to mark the tercentenary of the first play. Similarly the 350th anniversary was marked in 1984 by a special series of Plays.

The Pedlar with his Carvings

The Setting

The Ammergau Valley has been an important communications route for centuries. In Roman times it lay on the military route from Verona to Augsburg, and in common with most of the passable routes across the Alps, it has been fought over time and again. Thus it has been in the hands of many different rulers, but most importantly a part of the lands of the Dukes of Bavaria, culminating with the rule of the famous 'mad' King Ludwig II, a friend of Wagner and builder of those fairy tale castles . Ludwig was a great benefactor to the village and his name is still revered and remembered, especially on his birthday, August 25th, when the mountain-sides are lit up with bonfires and fireworks.

The village stands some 840 metres above sea level, in a valley almost totally surrounded by mountains. It is approached from the east by a road which winds its way up from the autobahn between Munich and Garmisch-Partenkirchen. The other main road out takes a northerly direction, following the river Ammer through the 'twin' village of Unterammergau, and then to Schongau and north towards Augsburg.

Coming from the east the road passes through the village of Ettal, with its huge monastery and fine church founded in 1330. Oberammergau was administered from here for many years, and the Monastery and its incumbents have always had a great influence on the Passion Play, as we shall see later. Together with its fellow monastic institutions at Rottenbuch and Steingarden, Ettal forms a geographical triangle, in the southern corner of which, known as Priests Corner, Oberammergau lies.

In its trade route days, the people of Oberammergau made a good living from providing transport and lodgings for the traveller. In the winter months they busied themselves by making wooden toys and utensils, the foundation of the woodcarving art for which Oberammergau is famous today. Those who lived in the mountains developed the art especially well, since they could not move far from their homes once the snows had descended, and the animals were kept in the warmth of their farmhouses. They would spend the winter carving toys, religious figures and household utensils, and when summer arrived some would set off to peddle their wares in the surrounding area. The goods were carried on a large wooden frame, slung over the back. A carved representation of such a pedlar is one of the attractive sights of the village centre today.

Of the surrounding mountains two in particular stand out. The Laber, on the eastern edge of the village, is 5600ft high and can be ascended by cable car from the village. On the southern edge of the village is the Kofel (4480ft), a sugar loaf shaped mountain with a great cross on its peak. This is often used as a symbol of the village and it is on the slopes of the Kofel that many of the traditional festivities of the village take place, such as the torchlight procession on the birthday of King Ludwig II.

12

A Tour of the Village

Most of those who arrive in Oberammergau to see the Passion Play will come as part of a wider tour of which the Play is a climax, and they will spend at most two nights in the village. As virtually the whole of one day is taken up by the play itself, there will be little time for exploration in the village and its surroundings. This is a great pity, for there is much to see which is of interest and beauty, but hopefully the first brief visit will act as a stimulant to come again another year and stay for a longer spell. Oberammergau does in fact make an excellent centre for a holiday at any time of the year. It has excellent winter sports facilities, and in non-Passion Play years more visitors will come in winter than in summer. There are a number of ski-lifts, a chair lift to the Kolbensattel and the cable car to the Kofel mentioned in the last chapter. There are several good ski runs and the area is also popular for cross-country runs into the Graswang valley. One famous run, "In the footsteps of King Ludwig" is some 65 km long. Then, of course, there are the Olympic standard facilities of Garmisch-Partenkirchen, which is only about 12 miles away.

The village centre is compact with just two main streets containing the shops, banks and other facilities, including the **Museum**. Your Passion Play arrangement will almost certainly allow you free entrance to this, and it is worth seeing for the splendid collection of finely carved Christmas Cribs. Wax carving is another of the arts of the village and this, too, is well represented, as finely worked wax candles are a popular souvenir of the village.

But the main visual attraction of the village will be the decorated **Frescoes** on many of the houses. This is an art which goes back more than 200 years. Known in German as luftlmalerei, it is quite common throughout Bavaria and in parts of the Austrian Tyrol, but nowhere so abundant as in Oberammergau. The oldest frescoes date from around 1768, the date on one on a chemist's shop in Dorfstrasse, and were by Franz Zwink. He died in 1792 and his works mainly depict Biblical scenes or the lives of the saints. Some of the finest examples are on the building known as Pilate's House, which is now municipally owned and used for exhibitions. Others of note are on the Hansel and Gretel House, an orphanage on the edge of the village centre towards Ettal. You will be able to recognise many of the nursery rhyme characters – Puss in Boots, Rumpelstiltskin and many more. Other frescoes are more modern but they are plentiful and add a great deal to the attraction of the place.

The shops themselves will be a great attraction, especially those which are dedicated to the art of the **Woodcarver**. Several carvers have their studios open to view and you can sometimes see them at work and purchase the

Facing Page: *Frescoed houses of Oberammergau*

results. You may even recognise some of them as actors in the Play. The quality of the carving does of course vary, but almost all the examples you will see will be hand carved in the village, not machine turned and imported. It follows that they will not be cheap. The village in fact supports almost 500 practising wood carvers, and there is a well-known carving school, in Ludwig Lang Strasse (on the road towards the cable car station) which is sometimes open to the public. It has an international reputation and occasionally mounts exhibitions, though in Passion Play years most of the students will be engaged in the Play.

The Parish Church is dedicated to the Blessed Virgin Mary and the Apostles Peter and Paul. It was built between 1736 and 1742 and is a fine example of the Rococo period with a marvellously ornate interior in white and gold. There is, as you would expect, some fine carving, as well as ceiling paintings, which all create a wonderfully light atmosphere. If you are fortunate enough to attend a service, you will find that the standard of music matches the quality of the surroundings, The fine organ is used for teaching local children and is part of the great emphasis which is placed on music and drama in local education. Fittingly, all the arts of Oberammergau find expression here. You may hear the organ being played in the afternoons, after the Play performances, and Mass will be celebrated each evening .

The Protestant (Lutheran) Church is a more modern structure, situated close to the Passion Play Theatre. It also has daily services with Holy Communion during the Passion Play season

In Eugen-Papst Strasse you will find a building, which has been provided from the proceeds of previous plays. This is the **Ammergauer House**, a kind of community centre, which includes an outdoor theatre, a concert hall, and restaurant, as well as the local **Tourist Office**. If you would like to see where the profits from other plays have been spent, you might pay a visit to the **Wellenberg Recreation Centre**, which is near the cable car station for the Laber. Here you will find several swimming pools, indoors and out, sauna, solarium, wave pool and water chutes.

This is an area of great scenic beauty and since the village is, as we have said, virtually surrounded by mountains, much of it can be seen from below. But if you do have time, try to take to the hills. An after dinner walk across the river and along King Ludwig Strasse offers a panoramic view and an easy climb to the **'Kreuzigungs Gruppe'**, a 40ft high stone monument depicting the Crucifixion. This was presented to the village by King Ludwig to mark his visit to the play in 1870. It was erected in 1875, but not without cost, as one of the labourers was killed when the statue of St John fell on him. There are many other marked paths, either from the Laber or the lower slopes of the Kofel to which access is from the road towards Ettal.

Facing Page: *Pilate's House*

The Play

Its organisation, administration and traditions

The village of Oberammergau has a population of around 5000 people, a figure which has changed very little in recent decades. Of these, something like 2000 are directly involved in the production of the Passion Play, either on stage or behind it, in the orchestra or chorus, or dealing with scenery, costumes and 'props'.

Since the rest of the population is largely involved in the business of catering for the 4700 people, plus coach drivers, tour escorts and other staff, who arrive for each performance, coming and going four times a week, it is easy to understand the impact which the Play makes upon the community, and to realise that it also creates some special problems in carrying on with every day life, jobs and careers, and especially when this disruption happens only for one year in ten. There is only a minute permanent staff retained for the interim years, though the business of tourism does provide many jobs all year round, but for most it is a matter of 'business as usual', not only in the years when there is no Play, but also during the Play season itself. For example, one of the leading actors in the 1990 play told us how he had used up all his annual leave and then had to take extra, unpaid, time off, in order to be able to fulfill his role on stage, and still keep his employer happy!

The handling of visitors is a huge operation in itself. For most performances, those on Mondays, Wednesdays and Fridays, tickets are sold as part of a package which also includes two nights accommodation, with dinner and breakfast, plus lunch on the day of the Play, use of local transport, and entrance to the Museum and various other facilities. Those attending the Play on Sundays will stay for just the one (Saturday) night. The accommodation is necessary because the play takes up most of one day, starting at 9am and ending around 5.30pm, with a three-hour break for lunch. Additionally, most visitors will come from some distance away, travelling as part of an organised tour and arriving by coach, so that parking for these vehicles is an operation on its own. There are also performances on Saturdays for which tickets are sold without an accommodation package – these are designed mainly for people who live within easy travelling distance of the village.

Because the number of hotels is limited, much of the accommodation is provided in private homes. It has long been a tradition in the village for people to open up their houses to visitors to the Passion Play, and for many visitors it is one of the delights of the visit to share the home of a typical resident. Many will also find that they are staying with a family at least one member of which is taking part in the Play, even possibly a leading member of the cast. It is almost certain that the host family will have some connection with the performances, if only as a member of the chorus. But even with this, Oberammergau is still not large enough to accommodate everyone, and some will find they are staying in a nearby village, such as Unterammergau or Ettal.

All this coming and going gives the impression, during the Play season, of a constantly mobile population, for whilst 5000 people live and work here, an almost equivalent number are either arriving or departing on 5 days of the week. The only periods of comparative peace and quiet are during the performances themselves, but even then there are constant comings and goings, for many of the cast will have walk-on parts during the bigger scenes and only need to be there for small parts of the Play. In between times, they can get on with their normal lives, running their businesses or homes. The day of a typical hausfrau might begin at dawn with the housework and preparation of breakfast for her guests. Then it is down to the theatre office to hand in arrangement coupons for her guests (otherwise she won't get paid) or handing in tickets for any that have not shown up. By 9am she might well be in costume, on stage as part of the great opening scene, the 'Entry into Jerusalem, and then it is back home to start preparing lunch for, perhaps, four or six guests as well as her own family. She will probably have to return to the theatre, put on her costume again for another scene, before she needs to get dinner ready to serve by 7 o'clock.

There are a total of 130 speaking parts, plus a host of smaller parts for players in the crowd scenes, or Roman soldiers. The total size of the casts is more than 1000 and there is an orchestra of over 50 players, and a chorus of similar proportions. At one point there can be as many as 600 people on stage at a time, and with all of the back stage and 'front of house' staff, it can readily be seen that the scale of the operation is tremendous, indeed for sheer size of production, the Oberammergau Passion Play is unequalled anywhere.

We must not forget the animals that take part, the sheep, the doves and, of course, the donkey ridden by Jesus into Jerusalem. There is as much pride in selection among the owners of these as there is for the human parts.

The production is steeped in traditions, though some of them have been gradually eroded with the passing of time. To take part, a person must have been born in the village or lived there for at least 20 years. At the end of the Second World War there was a considerable influx of refugees from Eastern Europe, which expanded the population quite significantly. They were assimilated successfully and became eligible to take part in the Play from 1970. Any child who attends the local primary school can also take part, whatever his or her nationality or birthplace, and there are quite a number of service families in the village from the various NATO nations as that body has an establishment there.

The production also eschews such modern contrivances as microphones, make-up, wigs, lighting effects or amplification. Needless to say, the acoustics in the auditorium have to be excellent, and they are. But it also means that a large proportion of the male population must grow beards, indeed many are permanently bearded. Traditionally, men cease shaving on Ash Wednesday in the year before the Play, but some may have to shave in the end if they are selected to play Roman soldiers, for they are always clean shaven. In fact, neither lighting nor make-up would be of much benefit since the Play is performed on an open stage, but the intention is to produce the closest possible resemblance to the original Biblical characters.

It is the traditions relating to women that have caused the most controversy, especially in recent years. The original position was that no woman could take part who was either married or over the age of 35. Since the text requires some 295 women on stage, that has always been a difficulty, but for generations past, many marriages have been postponed, often for years, in the hope of the bride-to-be being chosen to play Mary, Magdalene, or one of the other major female parts. For the 1990 Play, it was decided, but not without much controversy, that married women would no longer be barred, and in fact one of those selected to play Mary was the cause of a headline in a British Sunday newspaper, 'Virgin Mary is mother of two'. For the 2000 Play, the age limit of 35 for women has also been discarded, the result of sex-discrimination legislation in Germany.

The Play is the "property" of the community of Oberammergau as expressed through its Town Council, and the Council takes all decisions relating to it. It is supplemented in the year prior to each Play by those appointed as Director, Deputy Director, and Director of Music, together with the Catholic priest and the local Lutheran Pastor to form the Passion Play Committee. It is the Council which has to put up the considerable capital which is needed to finance each production – 13 million Deutchmarks are being spent on the Theatre rebuilding alone for the 2000 series – and that represents a huge debt for so small a community. A great deal also has to be spent on the infrastructure needed to cope with the influx of visitors, car parks, toilets, drainage and sewerage systems, all of which have to be upgraded and renewed on a continuous programme of works.

Profits from the Play have always been ploughed back into facilities for the benefit of the community, residents and visitors alike. Outstanding among these is the Wellenberg recreation centre, with its indoor and outdoor alpine swimming pools, and the Ammergauer House, a Community Centre which includes a theatre and concert hall, as well as a restaurant. The village also boasts a Thermal Clinic for the treatment of rheumatic diseases, and a new Rehabilitation Centre has recently been added. Education is very important, and especially music and drama, into which a great deal of money is poured. Every child is encouraged to take up these arts and those who show talent are given every opportunity to progress, for they are the future of the Passion Play.

The Entry Into Jerusalem (1990)

There is some reticence when the question of remuneration for the actors is raised. They are, of course, all amateurs and no one is paid a salary as such. But nowadays it is clearly impractical to expect people to give up such a huge proportion of their lives to the Play and suffer loss of income in addition. So players are given an allowance to compensate for loss of earnings. Looking around the village one has the impression that there are no paupers, but it is equally clear that no one makes a fortune from it either, so one has to assume that they have the balance just about right.

The Passion Play Theatre

There has been a theatre on the present site, dedicated solely to the Passion Play, since 1830. Prior to that, the Play was staged on several other sites in halls and theatres in the village, but originally of course, in the Churchyard. The 1830 theatre had seats for 5000 people, all in the open air, The present theatre was built for the 1900 plays and seated 4200, but it was extended when the stage was rebuilt in1930 to provide seating under cover for 5200. This number has subsequently been reduced to comply with modern fire and safety regulations and the present capacity is 4700.

For the 2000 play series, a vast re-building scheme has been undertaken at a cost of some DM13Million. New seats have been put in and under floor heating has been installed, so comfort should be considerably improved, no small factor when the audience sits there for some five and a half hours, albeit with a long lunch break. The theatre will be provided with a new façade and considerable improvements are also being made to the back-stage area and technical equipment.

The Theatre Stage

The theatre is hardly architecturally impressive, either inside or out, though the recent improvements will make a difference. It gives something of the impression of a large barn, with its web of iron girders over plain walls, which are now made of a fireproofed timber. The walls are covered with canvass hangings during performances, but the rather stark appearance does provide the remarkable acoustical properties which are such that every word spoken on stage can be heard anywhere in the theatre without any recourse to microphones or loudspeakers.

Today's audience is, as we have said, comfortably seated under cover, but the stage remains open to the elements, and the Play continues virtually whatever weather conditions can throw at it. Snow, storms and floods have been known to interrupt it, though very rarely, but the setting of the stage, with its backdrop of gently rising slopes, the more distant mountains, and (with a little bit of luck) a few clouds scudding across a clear blue sky, must be one of the most impressive for any theatrical performance to be found anywhere. Those occasions when thunder and lightning punctuate the performance may not be comfortable for the actors and musicians, but can add even more dramatic effect to the story. Thus the location provides its own scenery and the stage needs to be embellished only by the simplest of effects. The porticos of Pilate's House, on the left, and the House of the High Priest, on the right, are the main elements, with the arches between them representing the entrances to the streets of Old Jerusalem. The front of the stage becomes the area in front of the Temple, where the main action of the Play takes place.

There is a central stage to the rear, which is covered and has side walls of glass. It is here that the Old Testament Tableaux are prepared and presented, as well as some of the scenes of spoken drama. The scene has to be shifted some 40 times during each performance, and this requires a considerable amount of technical equipment, including a moveable stage and a drop stage, so that scenes can be prepared below and then hoisted up and rolled forward quickly and almost noiselessly, as they are needed, for there are no curtains to be drawn to hide this action as in a normal theatre. There are also electrically driven scene cloths to the central stage, which are wound on to huge steel rollers below.

Behind the stage are the 16 wardrobe rooms, which house over 1000 costumes. Many of them are extremely old and valuable, some intricately embroidered, and their maintenance is a continuous task for a small permanent staff. All the costumes are made in the village and some are replaced for each series. Also back stage are the rooms where many items of stage equipment, or "props", are stored. Some of these are very old – the table and stools used in the Last Supper scene, for instance date back over 200 years. The heavy wooden cross, which is used in the Crucifixion scene, has to be fitted with special devices to hold the actor secure for the 20 minutes this scene lasts; similarly the crosses of the malefactors. Prior to 1990 the Cross of Jesus was

Woodcarver Karl Führler at work in his studio – he plays the part of a High Priest in the 2000 play

larger than the other two, but now they are all three the same height. There is a smaller, more portable cross which is used for the Journey to Calvary scenes.

During non-Passion Play Play years, the theatre itself is open to the public and you can tour the back stage area and costume rooms. An exhibition showing the history of the Play is put on. Guided tours in several languages are conducted several times a day.

Facing Page: *The Crown of Thorns (1990)*

The Practical Details

Performances

The schedule of performances for the 2000 series of Plays runs from May 22nd to September 29th. (but see note regarding one day arrangements, below) with the Play being put on every Monday, Wednesday, Friday and Sunday. Tickets for all of these performances are sold only as part of an arrangement which also includes accommodation. Those attending the Monday, Wednesday and Friday plays will stay in the village two nights, whilst those seeing the Sunday performance will have one night's accommodation included.

In addition, there will be performances on each Saturday from May 27th to September 30th and one Sunday performance, on October 1st, which will not include any accommodation, but ticket sales are restricted to those who live within easy travelling distance. Thus a total of 95 performances will be given, with a total capacity of almost half a million people.

Timing

The performance commences at 9am each day and will finish at around 5.30pm. There is a lunch break of about 3 hours. Those with accommodation arrangements have lunch included and will take it either at their accommodation address or at a local restaurant.

Tickets & Arrangements

As stated above, the arrangements for Monday, Wednesday and Friday performances will include two nights' accommodation with dinner and breakfast, plus lunch on the day of the performance. The coupon will also allow access to local public transport, as well as to and from the point of arrival/departure, e.g. the local railway station, and between your accommodation and the theatre. It also includes entrance to the local Museum and to an exhibition on the history of the Passion Play, which will be staged in Pilate's House. A copy of the Text Book of the Play is also included (available in English).

For the Sunday performance, guests will arrive in the village on Saturday evening and depart after the performance ends.

Virtually all the tickets and arrangements are sold out many months in advance, but a few are kept back for sale on the day of the performance, and these, together with any returned or not taken up, are sold from a kiosk in front of the theatre on the morning of the performance. But the demand is likely to far outstrip the supply, and large queues are sure to form.

Accommodation & Prices

Prices for the arrangements depend upon the category of accommodation provided. This can vary from simple private homes, rooms with hot and cold water, via pensions, small hotels to larger and very smart hotels. Including a 10% booking fee (which is charged even by the Play Committee if you book direct) they start at DM358.60 for the lowest category, one night arrangement, rising to DM819.50 in the highest category hotels for a two night stay.

All the arrangements, except those in the lowest category, include a first class seat for the Play. The second class seats (those on the side aisles) go with the simple private house accommodation. First class seats are in the centre of the theatre, but may be anywhere from front to back and there is no possibility of choice in terms of location.

For the Saturday performances (and for Sunday October 1st) which do not include accommodation, the prices for the Play will be DM165 for a first class seat, and DM 110 for second class.

How to Book

Those wishing to make their own arrangements should apply well in advance, first asking for an order form, which has to be completed and sent with the arrangement price. The address is as follows;

Geschaftsstelle der Passionsspiele 2000
Eugen-Papst Strasse 9a,
D-82487 Oberammergau
Germany
Telephone ++49/88 22/9231-0   Telefax: (0) 88 22/92 31-90

Details are also on the Internet: http://www.oberammergau.de   or you can make contact by e-mail at : tourist-info@oberammergau.de

Tourist Information

The local Tourist Office is in the same building in Eugen-Papst Str as the Passion Play office and is open daily from 9am to 12noon and from 2pm to 4pm, (closed Friday afternoon) but during the Play season it will be open from 8am to 7pm. The telephone No is ++49 88 22/10 21

Church Services

Both the Catholic Parish Church and the Protestant (Lutheran) Church will hold daily services in the village during the Passion Play season and offer a warm welcome to those of all denominations. Organ music will be played in both churches during the afternoons, and Holy Communion will be celebrated in the Protestant church at 5.30 pm and 9pm each day. Mass will be celebrated in the Catholic Church at 6pm and 7.30pm. A leaflet entitled 'The Churches Invite You' will be widely available in the village.

The Ecumenical Centre

This is run by a team of English speaking Ministers under the auspices of the British Council of Churches. They will welcome groups on arrival and give a preparatory talk on the evening before the performance of the Play. The team includes a Roman Catholic priest, but comes under the administration of the Anglican Diocese for Europe. The Centre can be found at the Catholic Parish Hall on the corner of Hillernstrasse and Herkul-Schwaiger Str, quite near the Parish Church.

How to get there

By Air

The majority of those coming by air will arrive at Munich International Airport, which is at Freising, about 17 miles NE of the city. Travelling time between the airport and Oberammergau will be around two hours, and a special bus service will be laid on for the duration of the season. Many others will, of course, use airports in Austria and other neighbouring countries if they are visiting Oberammergau as part of an inclusive tour which also takes in other centres.
If you are flying from within Germany it is worth considering services to Augsburg airport, which is around 65 miles from Oberammergau. Augsburg Airways serves six other German cities and there are car hire facilities at the airport.

By rail

German Railways (DB) will have special through-trains from a number of departure points including some of the channel ports. Details can be obtained from the international offices of DER Travel. The London Office is at 18 Conduit Street, WIR 9TD (Tel: 020-7317-0919). In New York they are at 780 Third Avenue NY 10017 (Tel: 212-754-9100) , and there is also an office in Chicago (Tel: 847-430-5771). All trains will run via Munich, from where there will be a regular supplemented service into Oberammergau.

By car

The distance from the Channel ports is approximately 600 miles, depending on the route you take and your port of arrival. It will be virtually all motorway/autobahn standard, and there are no tolls for using the autobahns in Germany. The most direct route is via Brussels and Aachen, using the A61, which bypasses Koblenz and Ludwigshafen. but you can detour to see the most scenic part of the Rhine Valley between Koblenz and Mainz (or better still take a river boat if you have time). Boppard, Rudesheim, the Lorelei and Bingen are the highlights. If you take the A6 via Heilbronn towards Stuttgart it will be fast, but also furious, and again if you are in no hurry, try the very scenic Neckar Valley from Heidleberg to Heilbronn. From south of Stuttgart you can either follow the A6/E11 to Munich, and then the autobahn south toward Garmisch-Partenkirchen, or go south from Augsburg, which is a more scenic run. Another alternative is to stop at Ulm, on the river Danube, to see its magnificent Gothic Cathedral, with the world's tallest spire (528ft). Autobahn A7 will take you most of the way south from there.

Depending on your approach route you could either stop and see the Church at Wies or the Monastery at Ettal, (see page 34) before getting to Oberammergau.

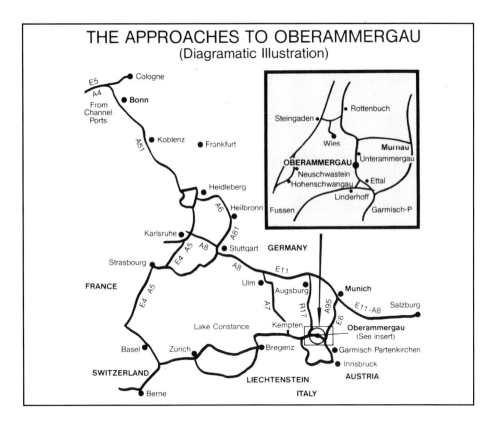

THE APPROACHES TO OBERAMMERGAU
(Diagramatic Illustration)

Visits in the surrounding area

The Legacy of King Ludwig 11

The famous 'mad' King Ludwig the Second of Bavaria has received his fair share of attention over the years, through film and television, and the numerous fantasies about his life and death, are well documented. He was born in 1845, the son and heir to Crown Prince Maximillian and Princess Marie of Prussia. His childhood was spent mainly at the Castle of Hohenschwangau, which stands below the mountainside on which he was later to create his most famous fantasy – Neuschwanstein. From an early age his artistic flair was apparent and he was always devoted to painting, with a love of romantic legend, and to music. At the age of 16 he met Richard Wagner, who became his trusted and valued friend. Ludwig was one of the great patrons of the arts, and he supported Wagner in particular with unbounded generosity. But the finest legacy he has left for us to enjoy are the three magnificent castles which, together with Hohenshwangau itself, are within easy reach of Oberammergau either as a day excursion, or perhaps to visit on the way to or from the Passion Play village.

The most distant is the Castle of **Herrenchiemsee**, which is situated on an island in the centre of the huge Chiemsee Lake, between Munich and Salzburg – it can be seen from the A8 autobahn. Ludwig had become King of Bavaria at the early age of 18, and from the beginning his reign was one of contrast. On the one hand he sought to modernise his kingdom, not only through the arts, but also by the provision of rather more down to earth facilities such as schools and hospitals There is no doubt that he was greatly loved by his people and is remembered even today with affection, especially in Oberammergau where they celebrate his birthday annually with bonfires, fireworks and parades. All this in spite of the profligacy with which he spent money on a disastrous three-week war with the Prussians and on the lavish construction of his fairy tale castles.

The Castle at **Linderhof** is only about eight miles from Oberammergau and is a visit you should make if at all possible. It is on the other side of the mountain range which starts with the Kofel, and was inspired by the King's stay during his childhood at Versailles. It is a miniature masterpiece, built to serve merely as a hunting lodge, but its interior is very reminiscent of Versailles, even down to a Hall of Mirrors, and the whole is beautifully furnished and decorated in Baroque style. The gardens, too, are splendidly laid out, with a great fountain, lakes and an artificial 'blue grotto', complete with illuminations and a gilded shell-like boat. The great cascade of a waterfall at the rear of the house is a splendid sight when

Facing Page: *The Neuschwanstein Castle (Courtesy German National Tourist Office)*

Linderhof Castle (courtesy of German National Tourist Office)

it is working in summer, and in the grounds there is also a Moorish Pavilion, recently removed from Oberammergau, where it was found in a dilapidated state and stylishly renovated. A longer walk will bring you to a Hunting Hut, which is decorated with scenes from Wagnerian operas. Visits within the castle can only be made with a guided group, and these are regularly done in English.

Hohenschwangau overlooks the village of the same name, a few miles from the border town of Fussen, itself the possessor of a great castle. There has been a castle on this site from the 12th century, but it lay in ruins from the 16th century until it was re-built by Ludwig's father, Maximillian, in the 1830's. Ludwig's childhood home contains many memories of his life. The castle is reached by steep stairs from the village street, and from its terraces (to which there is no entry fee), there are excellent views across the valley to the more famous Neuschwanstein and beyond. The interior of Hohenschwangau is richly decorated with paintings and frescoes, notably those of the 'swan knight,' Lohengrin, and the furnishings include some fine bronzes, carvings and crystal.

Close to the village centre are the two lakes, which also have romantic associations. The smaller one is known as Swan Lake (Schwansee), and the larger is the Alp lake (Alpensee). You can walk around both amidst majestic mountain scenery.

The best views, however, are to be obtained from the balcony of **Neuschwanstein Castle**, without doubt the jewel in Ludwig's crown. There had been an earlier castle on this site also, but Ludwig saw its elevated position as ideal for the realisation of his dreams, and work started in 1869. This

The Monastery at Ettal (courtesy of German National Tourist Office)

is probably the most photographed castle in Europe, the very epitome of the hackneyed term 'fairy tale', which is clearly why it was chosen to feature in the film 'Chitty Chitty Bang Bang'.

To reach the Castle from the village, you must take either a horse drawn carriage or a mini-bus. Even from where they drop you there are some 136 steps to climb to the entrance, and then you must wait until the next guided tour in English is announced. In summer these are very regular. But all this effort is well worth while, for the Castle is richly panelled and decorated, especially with paintings of the romantic era, many depicting scenes from Parsifal and Tannhauser, which are said to have inspired Wagner to write his Ring Cycle operas. Most opulent of all is the Singers Hall, where the paintings are by a trio of Munich artists, Spiess, Pitloty and Christian Jank. The latter was also responsible for much of the interior design in the castle. This room was curiously never used for concerts in Ludwig's lifetime, but it has since become a most favoured venue. Concerts have sometimes been staged by the light of 600 candles

The whole visit to Neuschwanstein and surrounding area really needs a full day. There is superb walking country around and within the grounds of the Castles. Especially dramatic is the Queen Mary Bridge, which spans a 300ft deep gorge close to Neuschwanstein. Those with time and energy can make a 3-hour walk to the top of the Tegelberg mountain, though there is also a cable car. There are plenty of restaurants and other facilities in Hohenschwangau village, which is the base for the visit.

A Map of the Village

Key

1 Catholic church
2 Town hall
3 Tourist Office
4 Passion play theatre
5 Evangelic church
6 Fire brigade
7 Museum
8 Railway station
9 Post office
10 Woodcarving school
11 Tennis & Squash courts
12 Catholic rectory
13 School
14 Rheumatic clinic
15 Cure clinic
16 Youth Hostel
17 Miniature golf
18 Swimming and recreation centre
19 Mountain railway centre
20 Chair lift
21 Sports ground
22 Pilate's house
23 Bundeswehr and NATO school
24 Reptile zoo
25 Camp site
26 Police

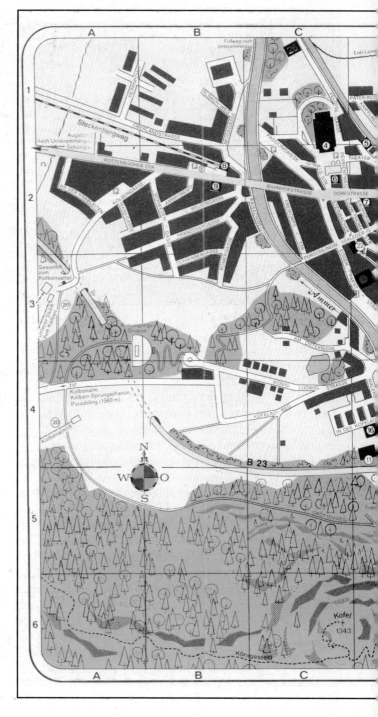

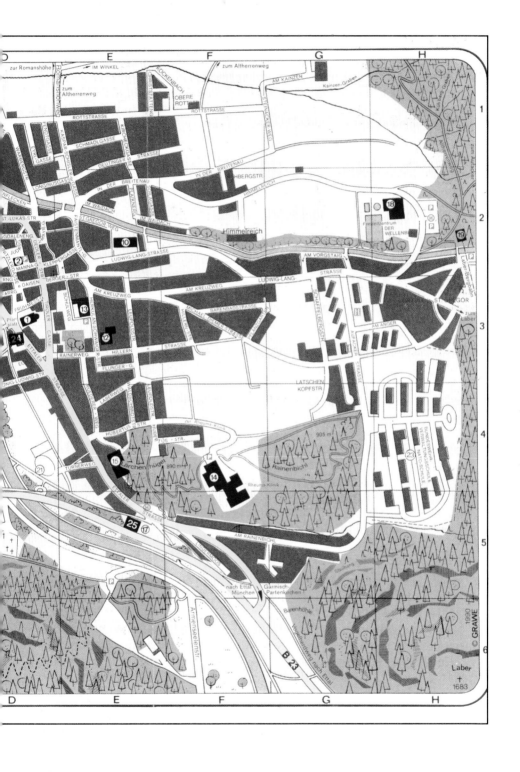

The Monastery at Ettal

Ettal is around 3 miles from Oberammergau on the road leading towards the Munich autobahn. It is dominated by the imposing edifice of the Monastery in the centre of the village. It was founded in 1330 by an earlier Ludwig and its inmates have long been associated with the Passion Play – in fact Oberammergau was at one time governed from Ettal. Much of the building, including a library of 30,000 books, was destroyed by fire in 1711. It was rebuilt, only to suffer again in the secular dissolution of 1803. The impressive Church, which is its centrepiece, is a fine example of rococo decoration and the Monastery also has both a brewery and distillery ,which produce a well-known liqueur. It also has a very good school, which in turn has a choir with a high reputation in the locality.

The Church at Wies

Down a lonely country road through forests, some 16 miles from Oberammergau, off the road from Rottenbuch to Steingaden, lies a farm, a church, and very little else. Standing almost alone, this great church is an important place of pilgrimage for Catholics from the world over. It is also one of the richest examples of rococo decoration to be found anywhere in Europe. Its reputation is built upon the legend of a statue of the Flagellated Saviour, which was felt to be so ugly that it was banned from the annual procession. It was left to rot in an attic of the nearby farmhouse, until one day the farmer's wife, doing some clearance work, had a vision of the statue dripping with real tears. This was in 1738, and news of the 'miracle of tears' spread so widely that the number of pilgrims coming to Wies rapidly increased and continual additions to the church could not cope with the crowds. Foundations of the present great church were laid in 1746, and the image of the Flagellated Saviour remains its centrepiece today. The quality of the white marble and the gilded decoration, together with the fine carving and impressive paintings and frescoes, combine to produce a marvellously light effect. The combined work of the master builder, the masons and the artist at the same time has not often been bettered. Wies should not, if possible, be missed.

Garmisch-Partenkirchen

Some 15 miles from Oberammergau, these twin towns, separated by a railway line, have become a by-word for winter sports. The Olympic stadia and ski-jumps, the ice rink and other facilities, have made it one of the most popular centres. In summer, surrounded by the mountains, and dominated by the Zugspitz (2900m) which you can ascend by mountain railway from the town centre, it makes a good centre for touring the area. It is an attractive town and excellent shopping centre, with a pleasant old town of narrow streets and wrought-iron signs. An especially good place for walkers, as there are many lifts and cable cars available close to the town.

Munich

Many travellers to the Passion Play will land at Munich Airport, and some may have the luck to spend a day or two in this vibrant capital of Bavaria. It is worth several days there, for there is plenty to see and do.

Munich was the seat of the Wittlesbach family for 700 years from the 13th century – they included Maximillian I, who was the first King of Bavaria (from 1806), and his son, Maximillian II, who made Munich one of the great art cities of Europe. His progeny, of course, included our friend Ludwig II, builder of those fine castles. The complex of great buildings known as the Residenze, in a variety of styles and from different eras, includes the Palace of the Wittlesbachs as well as the National Theatre, the Treasury and several other Museums.

Nearby, there is the world famous Glockenspiel Carillon at the 'new' Town Hall, which attracts the crowds at 11am each day. There is also the splendid late-Gothic Cathedral (Frauenkirche), which dates from 1488, as well as a number of other important Churches, like the 11th century St Michael's. All of this, and much more, is in a small, compact area which is easily walked, but further away there are numerous other Museums and Galleries, not to mention the parks, the largest of which is called the English Garden. The paintings in the Alte Pinakothek Gallery are regarded as one of the most important collections in Europe. On the edge of the city is the Nymphenburg Palace, set in a huge park with lovely gardens, which houses a superb art collection

There are also the stadia built for the 1972 Olympics, and the great halls dedicated to Munich's most famous product – beer. The annual Oktoberfest, actually held in September, consists of a three week frolic of eating and drinking which attracts people from all over the world.

Innsbruck and Tyrol

Holidays which include the Passion Play will often also include some time spent in the Austrian Tyrol, most of which is within an easy day's drive from Oberammergau. Wherever you stay, a visit to Innsbruck is a must, for this fine city is wonderfully situated in a valley with, seemingly, a sheer wall of mountains at the end of almost every street. The broad avenue, Maria Theresien Strasse, forms its main shopping street, running from the great Triumphal Arch, past the Column of St Anna, to the entrance to the old city, with its arcaded shops, finely made wrought-iron signs and great stone houses, with walls so thick that city defences were unnecessary. Inside the old city is the famous Golden Roof, a gallery constructed by the Emperor Maximillian in 1500 to serve as a Royal box from which to watch the jousting in the square below. Opposite is the Helblinghaus, originally Gothic but later covered with such magnificent Rococo ornamentation that it became known as the Wedding Cake. The City Tower, in the same square, provides a fine view from the top, and at the riverside entrance to the old town stands a 14th century inn, the Ottoburg, with a statue to the Tyrolean Freedom Fighters outside it. Across the road from that is another old inn, the Golden Adler, which had associations with Goethe and many other poets and musicians. Innsbruck was one of the centres from which the Habsburgs ruled a great chunk of Europe, and the Royal Palace, the Hofburg, was built by Empress Maria Theresa, mother of Marie Antoinette, in 1777. It has a splendid interior and across from it is the incredible Court Church, with enormous bronze statues of the real and imaginary ancestors with whom Maximillian I hoped to be buried, but wasn't. Next to that is the really interesting Tyrolean Folk Museum. Great views of Innsbruck and its surroundings can be had by climbing any of the surrounding mountain ranges, but from the hill of Bergisel (end of tramline 1), you can not only admire the view but also inspect the Olympic Ski Jump, from the top of which competitors look straight down into the graveyard of the lovely Wilten Church. Known as the Wedding Church for its popularity, this is yet another example of extravagant Rococo, probably the best in the Tyrol. At the other end of tramline 1, by the river, is the funicular to the Hungerberg, a small village on a plateau above the city. You can go still higher from here, by cable car to Seegrube, and the mountaintop at Hafelekar (7500ft). The panoramic view includes all of the surrounding mountains, which rise up to 13000 ft, across Innsbruck to resorts such as Seefeld, and to the great Europa Bridge, which leads to the Brenner Pass and Italy. Straight ahead across the valley is the "sun terrace" plateau below the Patscherkofel Mountain (6460 ft), surmounted by a radar tower, on the slopes of which the Olympic downhill races are run. On this sun terrace are the resort villages such as Vill, Igls, and Tulfes.

The Cable Car from Igls takes you to the top, and to the Olympic bobsleigh run, and some excellent walks and stupendous views. The start of the Stubai Valley can be seen, one of the most scenic rides, whether by road or the ancient electric tramway, only one of numerous excursions along the valleys which spread out from Innsbruck. The route from this area towards Garmisch and Oberammergau takes you over the Fernpass, one of the most scenic drives imaginable.

The Play and the People

The Creative Team

For the first time, the 2000 Passion Play will come under the direction of a specially created team of writers, designers, directors and musicians, who together have made significant, possibly revolutionary, changes to the text, the sound and the appearance of the Passion Play. The major innovation is the appointment of a Theological Advisor, in the person of **Professor Dr Ludwig Mödl**, a religious historian at Munich University. This may well be an attempt to anticipate and dispel any criticism of the kind that has surfaced in the past regarding the text, which American Jews in particular have previously claimed is anti-Semitic.

The Director will again be **Christian Stückl**, who was also made Director of the 1990 Play when he was only 28 years of age. At that time he wanted to introduce changes but with little time for manoeuvre, he was forced to stay with the traditional text. Now, ten years on, he has been able to introduce new colleagues and persuade the local committee that it is time to move on. It is always very difficult to balance the historic traditions of the basic story of the Passion of Christ, with the need to express a message which is meaningful for today. Prof. Mödl describes the result as 'not simply a piece of folk theatre, but a Play of release', which transmits hope for humanity in the future. Christian Stückl, a native of Oberammergau, has a high reputation as a theatrical director throughout Germany and in many other parts of the world. He has directed many Shakesperean productions, in Oberammergau itself and in Munich, but also in India and Vienna, and has also directed Ben Johnson and Christopher Marlowe. In the 1990 Passion Play he directed both his father and grandfather who had parts as Judas and Ananias respectively.

The revisions to the text have been in the hands of **Otto Huber**, the deputy, or second Director. He was born in Oberammergau in 1947 and also took the same role in 1990. He is a member of a family whose association with the Passion Play goes back as far as 1680. He himself has spoken the Prologue in 1990 and his grandfather, Huber Rutz, played Caiaphas three times, and Peter in 1950. Otto Huber is a teacher at the gymnasium at Murnau and has a great deal of experience in producing drama in the local area.

The Music for the 2000 Play has also undergone some alteration at the hands of the senior musical director **Marcus Zwink**. He has two assistants, Maria Buchwieser and Michael Bocklet, to share the conducting duties. Alterations to the text, and the Old Testament Tableaux in particular have required that some of the original music score by Rochus Dedler, which has been used since 1820, should be changed, sometimes to provide a new and more dramatic emphasis, for instance in the scene relating to the betrayal by Judas. Some use has been made of other music composed by Dedler, who

Design for the Last supper scene in 2000

though not well known outside Germany is nonetheless a composer of stature. Marcus Zwink teaches music at the Cloister school at Ettal and also directs the local choir and orchestra, which have recently produced a CD which includes Dedler's *Misa Solemnis*.

But perhaps the major changes which will be noticed in 2000 by those who have seen previous Passion Plays, will be the design of the sets, and especially those for the Old Testament Tableaux. These have been produced by **Stefan Hageneier**, another native of the village (he was born in 1972) who now works mainly in Munich, but has also designed productions in New York and many other German cities. His designs for such tableaux as those portraying, for instance, Daniel In the Lions Den, and Tobias and the Angel, are unequivocally modern. Hageneier took a part as an extra in 1990, and is a graduate of the Oberammergau Wood Carving School.

Whilst those who see the Passion Play for the first time in 2000 may not be aware of it, the alterations made from the 1990 and previous versions are very considerable (some 65% of the text has been re-written) and it remains to be seen what the critics will make of it. But it is clear that there has been a very real attempt to make the Passion of Our Lord relevant to the 21st century, and hopefully that will be transmitted to those who see it.

The Family Tradition

We have mentioned that Otto Huber, the deputy director, can trace his family connection with the Passion Play back to 1680, and he is by no means the only one to take part in the 2000 Play who will bear a proud family history of participation.

There is, for instance, the family Preisinger, who run the Alte Post Hotel in the village centre. The present owner, Anton Preisinger Jnr., took a small part in 1990, but his father, the late Anton Snr. was one of the most formidable figures of the village from 1950 , when he played Jesus, and again in the same part in 1960. He became Director for the 1970 play, and then took smaller parts in both 1980 and 1984. But theirs is recent history compared with the Zwinks. Marcus, as we have seen is the Musical director, but he is a descendant of Franz Seraph Zwink, the gifted Rococo painter who created most of the earlier frescoes on the houses in the village. The Zwinks go back at least as far as 1446, and it will be surprising if there are not several of them in the cast of 2000.

Another well known name is that of Lang. They have one of the proudest of family records, up to the time of Walter Lang, who played Nicodemus in 1990. They were also hoteliers, but are sadly no longer so. The family arrived in the village in 1723 and a Lang has played the part of Christ no less than 5 times, the last being Alois Lang in 1934. If there is no one called Lang in the cast for 2000, it will be the first time for several centuries. We have mentioned previously that Christian Stückl, the Director, follows both his father and grandfather in taking part, but both his name and that of Zwink were among the original signatories to the vow of 1633.

Selecting the cast

The selection of the Passion Play cast for the year 2000 took place in April 1999. It took the Council only a few hours to go through the procedure, but in fact it is a process which takes place over a long period, and it might even be said to be ongoing. We have mentioned previously the very strong tradition of music and drama in the community, and the great emphasis placed on the education of young people in the arts, with free tution and training. As you would expect, there is an active musical and artistic life in the village, and every year there are a number of productions of both religious and secular dramas, as well as concerts of every variety. All are keenly observed, as standards of performance will be noted and some will be invited in due course to apply for the various roles in the next Passion Play. Some of the drama productions are designated as training plays when these people make up the cast. So, by the time the selection process nears its climax, there is a general expectation of those who are likely to be the front runners for the major parts.

Since 1980 it has become the practice to choose two people for each of the

The Creative Team: Left to right: Christian Stückl (Director), Stefan Hageneier (Designer), Otto Huber (Second Director), Markus Zwink (Musical Director).

main roles, so that they take alternate performances. Previously there were understudies who also took minor roles, but asking any one person to undertake some 100 performances over a period of six months is to impose a great strain, especially if he or she is employed or in business. The selection of two people also has the advantage of deflecting media attention on those chosen for the major roles, Mary and Jesus in particular, as there is considerable effort made to avoid any aura of stardom being placed upon individuals. It had also been the practice to select a younger and a more mature person in each of the two main roles so that the two younger ones would play together and the two older people. But this was abandoned in 1990, and the selection is now based purely on ability. One of the odder effects of the previous ban on women over 35, was that it could sometimes mean that Mary was played by a woman who in real life was younger than the man playing her son!

Facing page: *Set design for Tobias and the Angel Tableau*

An introduction to
The Passion Play

The Text

The text used for several decades past has been basically that written by Alois Daisenberger, a former Priest in the village, for the 1850 production. The original play seems likely to have been borrowed from other Passion Plays then in existence, most notably in Augsburg, or from Welheim, where a Passion Play is known to have been performed in 1600 and 1615.

Between 1770 and 1800 the performance of Passion Plays was banned by decree, though Oberammergau did manage to obtain a dispensation on some occasions by making alterations to the text which passed the scrutiny of the censors. One Father Othmar Weis, who had remained at Ettal despite the dissolution of its Monastery, produced revised versions in the early years of the 19th century, and it was he, together with his pupil, Daisenberger, who saw the Play emerge from the secular era and brought it back to the full evangelistic spirit of the earlier years.

The text has seen many alterations since then, mostly minor in character, and is now rather shorter than it used to be. It has often been the centre of controversy, and has provoked many an argument, mainly of a rather pedantic theological nature, and latterly there have been claims from American Jewish bodies that the Play is anti-Semitic in character. They claimed that the text placed blame upon the Jews for the death of Christ. There were some references to the Jewish "guilt" which were removed in the 1970's and an alternative text was proposed for 1980 but rejected after a Referendum in the village. Such arguments will hardly affect the enjoyment of an English speaking audience, who will no doubt take the view that whatever may be done with words cannot alter the facts of history.

However, for the 2000 production, there will be major changes. As we have said in the chapter about the Creative Team behind the production, some 60% of the text has been re-written under the careful tutelage of Otto Huber. The intent has been to present a challenge to the audience to accept that the Passion of Jesus has a relevance to the present day. It will ask questions, rather than simply re-telling a story which is well known to all who see it. This has to be written before the new text has been published, and it will be interesting to see how it is received within the village, where the preservation of traditions has always been paramount.

Set design – Daniel in the Lions Den

The Chronology

The sequence of events in the Play is consistent with a harmony of the Four Gospels, but there are a number of scenes which, though inspired by the Bible story, are not actually scriptural, for instance the presence of Mary at Bethany, and her search for Jesus in Jerusalem. The role of the traders at the Temple in the conspiracy against Jesus, and the act of compassion for Him by Veronica, are given prominence. But these and other extra-Biblical scenes are skilfully woven into the drama of the Passion with telling effect.

The Characters

As we have shown, the text of the Play is by no means a continuous set of quotations from the Scriptures, but the words of the Bible are used with care and sensitivity within a text which is deeply spiritual and effectively captures the essence of the Gospel story.

Of the 130 characters with speaking parts, only about 30 are actually named in the Gospels. For instance, Nathaniel plays an important role as spokesman for the Priests. But this is, of course, not the Nathaniel who was one of the twelve Disciples, and as he appears in the Play he is not a character from the Bible at all. Nevertheless, all the characters, real or imaginary, faithfully reflect the tensions, the loyalties, the fears and the courageous devotion, which so marked those momentous days. The manner in which the triumph over the grave is brought to us in the final scenes remains ones of the most moving experiences one can have.

TheTableaux Vivants

These are 'living', though static, scenes depicting stories from the Old Testament, which are staged between the Acts of the living Play. They serve both to hold the attention whilst the scenery is being changed, as there are no curtains to be drawn, and also to provide a parallel link to the New Testament story. They are accompanied by music, and usually by the chorus or soloists.

These Tableaux have been an integral part of the performance since the 18th century, when they were introduced as an aid to prayerful meditation, for at that time they were intended to be seen in silence. They are intended also to reveal a basic truth of human experience and divine revelation, and it is through them that Directors have been best able to express their individuality. For that reason they have often been changed, as many will be for the 2000 Play, and the reader is directed to the Synopsis which follows to see how each Act is preceded by a Tableau which is relevant to the story that follows. As an example, the scene of the Last Supper is preceded by Tableaux which depict (a) The Manna in the Wilderness (Ex.16), to show the Breaking of the Bread, and (b) by the bringing of grapes from the Promised Land (Num.13), to illustrate the Sacrament of the Cup.

The Music

The musical score is treated with the same kind of reverence as is accorded to the text, and any alteration to it will be a matter for heated debate. But again, for the 2000 Play, there will be alterations, many of them necessitated by the amendments made to the script and the tableaux.

A locally born composer, Rochus Dedler (1779-1822), composed the present musical score in 1816. He was a teacher, choirmaster and organist in the village and achieved considerable fame as a composer. He was a favourite at the Court in Munich. Although he is best remembered for his music for the Passion Play, he has many other compositions of note to his name, and some more of his music will be used in 2000 to supplement the original. The present score is in an edition produced by Eugen Papst, another Oberammergau-born musician of some note, who was a friend and colleague of Richard Strauss.

Dedler was the first to introduce music to the Play, initially with a few vocal and orchestral items, but for the 1815 Play (there was just one performance that year) he produced a full score. The manuscript of it was destroyed in a large fire which swept through part of the village in 1818, and Dedler had to write it all again in time for 1820. His music has now been a strong feature of the Play for 180 years and it is difficult to imagine the production without it. Even with the alterations proposed for 2000, much of the original score will remain. Certainly it is tuneful and easy on the ear and many would think it deserves a wider hearing, but perhaps it is only within the context of the action on stage that the sensitive contributions of orchestra, choir and soloists can properly make their mark.

The Stage Sets

As we have mentioned earlier, this is yet another area in which dramatic change will be seen in 2000. There have been a number of previous designers, including Georg Johann Lang, who produced the Play from 1930 to 1960, when the sets were so decrepit that a new start had to be made. Controversy raged again at the sets proposed by a graduate of the Wood Carving School, Alexander Kraut. This led to the voting out of the then Director and his eventual replacement by Christian Stückl in 1990. But Stückl had to accept designs based on those of Lang for the 1990 Play, and it is only for the new millennium that he has been able to bring in new blood and fresh ideas.

These come from Stefan Hageneier, who also graduated at the Wood Carving School, and who will be just 28 when the 2000 production is staged. As will be seen from the designs we have illustrated, he will be introducing a great deal more colour, and much more drama into the sets, with some very contemporary interpretations of Biblical scenes.

The whole production in 2000 will cause a good deal of comment, create a huge amount of interest, and no doubt stir up controversy yet again, among the local people and those who have seen and loved previous Passion Plays. It will certainly have more movement, more drama, more colour, than previous Plays, yet central to it will be the message of the Passion retained from previous centuries, that Jesus Christ died for all of us.

Meet the Cast

The major actors for the Passion Play 2000 were selected in April 1999. As previously explained, it has become the practice to select two people to share the major roles, so as to avoid too much disruption to their normal lives. The cast will be as follows :

Teller of the Prologue: Otto Huber and **Stefan Hageneir**, who are respectively also the Deputy Director and Designer of the Play

CHRIST: Anton Burkhart, 29, who played Nathaniel in 1990 and comes from a family with a long tradition of taking part. He works as a forester.

Martin Norz, who also took the role in 1990. He is a Local Government Officer, who deals with town planning matters at the Town Hall.

Anton Burkhart

MARY: Elisabeth Petre, who works in a local gift shop, made history in 1990 by becoming the first married woman to take the stage. She plays the role of Mary for the second time.

Andrea Hecht runs an art shop locally with her sister. She is also married.

Andrea Hecht

MARY MAGDALENE: Ursula Burkhart, (37), a children's nurse, played Mary in both 1990 and 1984.**Helga Stuckenerger,** (38), took the same part in both 1990 and 1984 – she is a wood carver

CAIAPHAS: Stefan Burkhart, (31), brother of Anton and Ursula, was Pilate in 1990, whilst **Peter Stückl**, father of Christian and son of Benedikt, continues the long family tradition. He was also Caiaphas in 1980 and 1984, Judas in 1990.

ANNAS (The High priest): Benedikt Stückl, now 76,made his first appearance in the Passion Play of 1930 and has played both Caiaphas and Herod as well as Annas. **Martin Wagner** (61), a wood carver, also follows a family tradition, having previously appeared 3 times as Judas, and as Caiaphas last time.

NATHANIEl: Matthias Müller, horticultural engineer and **Martin Müller,** a wood carver (not related).

RABBI ARCHELUS: Dominikus Zwink, solicitor and member of a famous "Passion Play family" – brother of a former Jesus and **Thomas Unruh.**

EZEKIEL: Markus Köpf, a student and **Johannes Müller**, a carpenter.

NICODEMUS: Christoph Fellner, an interior designer and **Helmut Schmidt** a forester.

JOSEPH of ARIMATHEA: Albert Rudhart, a member of the local Town Council who also runs a business which keeps the streets of Oberammergau clean and tidy; and **Helmut Fischer**, who played Christ in 1970, Herod in 1984 and Pilate in 1990. He is currently the Mayor of the District Council.

GAMALIEL: A new role in 2000, as one of the High priests who stood up for Jesus at his trial before the Council. It will be shared by two wood carvers, **Karl Führler**, and **Karl Härtle.**

JUDAS: Carsten Lück, spoke the Prologue in 1990 and as a carpenter has been involved in building the stage set; and **Anton Preisinger**, son of the pro-prietor of the Alte Post Hotel continues his own family connection.

PETER: Leonard Fischer, nephew of Helmut, and **Stephan Reindl**, leader of the Mountain Rescue Team, who played Christ in 1990.

JOHN : Simon Fischer, another member of a well-known family, and **Frederik Mayet**. Both are students

Martin Norz and Elisabeth Petre as Jesus and Mary in 1990

PILATE: Zeno Bierling, who keeps a drug store and **Walter Fischer** – father of Simon, brother of Helmut, a teacher in the High School.

HEROD: Hans Jablonka, a drugstore assistant and **Eric Schmid,** a hotelier.

SIMON of BETHANY: Karl Eitzenberger, another wood carver and **Werner Karl Härtle.**

A Synopsis of the Play
by Professor Ingrid Shafer, Official Translator of the text into English

Prelude: Jesus is called the Saviour of the world. Focus on divine forgiveness.

Tableau: In the cross of Jesus, humanity recovers the life lost in paradise *(all tableaux are accompanied by singers, chorus, and orchestra)*.

Prologue: A welcome to all, brother and sister Pilgrims, who are united in love around the Saviour who came into the lost world in response to Israel's call.

Musical Selections
Call to the Father to light the fire of love in those gathered. Follow the Saviour on the Way of the Cross.

PART ONE OF THE PASSION

ACT I - Jerusalem

Jesus enters Jerusalem, accompanied by a jubilant crowd. He drives traders and money changers out of the temple. *(The Temple was visited by pilgrims from the various Jewish tribes scattered throughout the Roman Empire. Sacrificial animals and other items could be bought on the premises, but only with local currency, hence the money changers.)*
  Several merchants protest. Jesus and crowd start to sing a traditional Jewish pilgrimage psalm, praising God.

Caiaphas, the High Priest (appointed by Pilate), challenges the authority of Jesus to act in the Temple. Jesus answers a question with a question and refuses to back down to Caiaphas or answer the original question. Instead he tells the parable of the dishonest, murderous tenants.

Children and crowd shout Hosanna, proclaiming Jesus the Messiah *(the term Messiah is interpreted as a ruler who will lead a successful Rebellion against Rome)*. Dariabas and Ezechiel order them to stop. They don't. Jesus presents a child to them as example. He and his followers leave.

Ezechiel, Nathaniel, and Archelus urge Caiaphas to have Jesus arrested for leading the people astray and undermining the foundation of their faith. Caiaphas counsels patience because Jesus has too many followers and a riot might result.

ACT II – Bethany – The Annointing

Prologue: Jesus is portrayed as generous healer and miracle worker who is willing to die for those he loves.

Tableau – 1: The Parting of Tobias. Tobit has faith that his son will be able to heal his blindness.

Tableau – 2: The abandoned Bride yearns mournfully for her Beloved. The Chorus assures her that her beloved will soon return.

Bethany. Disciples and friends wonder if Jesus is the promised one. They leave to tell others of the miracles they have witnessed. Jesus asks his disciples "Who do the people think I am?" They respond in various ways. Peter identifies him as the Messiah, the Son of the living God. Jesus calls him "Petros, the Rock," and then challenges all the apostles to proclaim the kingdom of God.

Jesus and his friends, including Lazarus, Magdalene, Martha, Thaddeus, and Andreas are visiting Simon of Cyrene at his home. Judas expects Jesus to be proclaimed King of Israel and liberate them from the Romans. The others agree. Jesus disagrees, but they do not understand.

Magdalene anoints Jesus with a very expensive oil, and Judas objects to the waste of money which could have been better spent on charity. Jesus defends Magdalene and predicts his death at the hands of the Romans. He describes his dying both as defeat and victory. Magdalene and John understand.

Peter suggests Jesus remain in the safety of this home, and Jesus calls him "Satan." When asked to bring peace, Jesus tells them that his mission is to spread division, adding that his disciples must deny himself, take up the cross and follow him. Whoever wants to save his life will lose it, but whoever loses his life for Jesus' sake, will gain it.

He then sings a spring song, a traditional psalm, to Magdalene and tells her that they will never again be together on earth. She responds with the passage from the Song of Songs: "Strong as death is love."

Judas and Thomas ask Jesus to make arrangements for their material welfare if he really intends to leave them. Jesus tells them to stop worrying about such mundane issues. Judas insists.

Mary, along with Josef, Simon, Jacob, Judas, and other relatives of Jesus come on stage. Mary is concerned and others accuse him of irresponsibility because he has not settled down and started a family.

Jesus tells them that they will weep and lament, but the world will rejoice. Eventually, sadness will be transformed into joy. He tells his mother that he must be led to slaughter. All leave except for Judas who says that he is tired of believing and hoping.

ACT III - The Journey to Jerusalem

Tableau – Moses, on his way down from Mount Sinai with the tablets, sees the people dancing round the golden calf and gathers those who have remained loyal to the Lord around himself.
Prologue: Describes Jesus, aflame with God's spirit, struggling for humankind, and like Moses, gathering those who love the Father with their whole soul.

In the meantime the choir of the ones who do homage to the golden calf can be heard.

Journey to Jerusalem. Jesus preaches the Beatitudes. His followers speak of his miracles. Archelus worries that he will cause a popular uprising, and Nathaniel accuses Jesus and his followers of having abandoned the God of Israel. Peter and Andreas assure him that they are good Jews. Jesus accuses them of hypocrisy. Nathaniel calls him a seducer, and Jesus retaliates by calling them whitewashed tombs, filled with decay.

The crowd shouts Hosanna and is chased out of the Temple court yards by a mob.

Caiaphas, Nathaniel, and others discuss ways of stopping Jesus from destroying the very foundation of their form of Judaism, and punishing him for his defiance and arrogance. Nicodemus and Gamaliel object. *(There were, at the time of Jesus, several Jewish groups whose adherents differed widely concerning essential issues, such as life after death).* The enemies of Jesus are afraid to capture him in public because of his large following.

Judas enters, and offers to lead them to Jesus. They are suspicious, but decide to accept the offer. Judas will be paid 30 pieces of silver, the price of a slave.

After Judas leaves, the others, over the passionate objections of Nicodemus and Joseph of Arimathea, decide that Jesus must die.

ACT IV - The Last Supper

Tableau
The Paschal Meal before the Exodus.
Prologue
Jesus and his friends celebrate the night when the Lord freed his people from Egyptian bondage to lead them into the promised land.
Passion Narrative
Moses' meal, filled with hope for the coming of Lord prefigures the meal that Jesus shared with his friends.
Musical Selection
A chorus of Israelites calls for liberation from Egyptian servitude.

Last Supper. As is common at a Passover seder, John, the youngest participant asks Jesus to tell the story of the Exodus. He does, and goes on to quote Isaiah's dark words of war, violence, and the lack of love. He speaks of the Last Judgement and the way the merciful will inherit the kingdom while those who have shown no mercy and did not recognise that we love God by loving the unlovable among us will go to eternal punishment.

Jesus then speaks the traditional Passover blessing over the wine. He tells his friends that he came from the Father and is about to go back to the Father but will return to the world. He then washes their feet and asks them to serve one another as he has served them. Together they pray the "Our Father".

After the foot washing he shares bread and wine with his disciples while anticipating and interpreting his death. This scene weaves together motifs of the Passover meal and allusions to the blood of the covenant, the crucifixion, and the heavenly banquet in the Father's kingdom. This moment is remembered by Christians whenever they participate in the Sacrament of Communion.

Judas leaves after Jesus has accused him of planning his betrayal, and Jesus and the others get ready to go to the Mount of Olives.

ACT V – The Mount of Olives

Tableau 1: The treachery of Amasa who greeted his rival Amasa with a kiss and killed him with a dagger by the rock of Gibeon.

Scene 1.
Judas and the other enemies are approaching. Judas tells them that they

will be able to recognize their quarry by his kiss.

Tableau.2 Moses in front of the burning bush.
Prologue: In despair, Jesus pleads with the Father to save him from the agony to come, but like Moses, he accepts God's will.
Musical Selection: Moses' terror is portrayed as he encounters the burning bush, God' s voice calling Moses, Moses' futile struggle against the Lord's command, his excuses, and his ultimate acceptance of the awesome responsibility to lead the People Israel out of Egypt.
Passion Narrative: Jesus is shown kneeling in the olive grove, screaming in terror, and yet, ultimately offering himself to the Father.

Scene 2.
Jesus and the disciples discuss the events to come. There is much confusion and misunderstanding. Thomas expects Jesus to crush his enemies. Jacob expects the Lord to protect him. John expresses his disappointment that Jesus did not save Israel. Andreas reminds Jesus that he and the others left everything behind, and wonders what they will receive in exchange. Peter asks where they should go. Jesus insists that he was born for this moment. Yet he fears what is to come. He tells the disciples that they will take offence at him, and that Peter will deny him. He also predicts that they will be persecuted for his sake and be filled with the Sprit of Truth when needed.

Jesus prays alone. The disciples have fallen asleep. Jesus pleads for mercy and yet is ready to accept God's will. He is almost overcome with the weight of humanity's sins.

An Angel appears and speaks for the Lord, asking Jesus to allow himself to be pierced and crushed by humanity's sins in order that salvation might reach unto the ends of the earth. Jesus accepts the charge.

Judas and rabble arrive, along with some of the priests. Judas hurries up to Jesus and kisses him. Peter strikes Malchus' ear with his sword, and Jesus heals the wound, after commanding Peter to put his sword away. He then gives himself up to be arrested.

Musical Selection
The Chorus sings of the coming battle of agony and we are reminded in a duet that the shackles on the hands of Jesus are ransom for our freedom.

PART TWO OF THE PASSION

ACT VI - Jesus before Annas

Mocking. Peter's Betrayal and Repentance

Prologue: Describes the nocturnal interrogation and compares Jesus to Daniel and Job, mocked, abused, suffering in silence.
Tableau 1: The Prophet Daniel in the Lion's pit, sentenced to death because he honoured his God. The Chorus sings that in the end, justice will be done, wherever the voice of truth is smothered and the powerful oppress.
Tableau 2: Job in misery, taunted by family and friends, bearing the torment patiently.

Before Annas
Peter and John are discussing the fate of Jesus in the courtyard of Annas' house. What will happen to Jesus? John and Peter exit. Annas and other Council members come on stage. They are anxiously waiting for Jesus to be brought before them. Councillors and temple guards arrive with their prisoner.

Annas interrogates Jesus, asking him what he has been teaching, and accusing him of misleading the people and pretending to be greater than Abraham. Jesus replies that Annas should question his audience, and one of the men slaps him for impudence. Annas accuses him of dissenting from the renowned teachers and denigrating the office of priests. He tells the priests that Jesus must die before the festival.

Judas becomes very agitated when he hears that Jesus will die. He hurries off when Annas dismisses his concerns.

Several members of the Temple guard and women are trying to keep warm by a fire, when Jesus is dragged toward them. Peter and John enter and are invited by the men to join them. John and Peter approach the fire. The guards decide to entertain themselves by manhandling and mocking their prisoner, calling him a king of fools, and spitting at him.

When Peter is accused of being one of the Nazarene's disciples, he vigorously and repeatedly denies even knowing Jesus, and finally tears himself loose.

Jesus is taken to Caiaphas to be arraigned. Peter deeply regrets his cowardly denial of his friend and teacher and promises that nothing will ever separate him from Jesus again.

ACT VII - The Interrogation and Condemnation by Caiaphas and The Despair of Judas

Tableau: Cain, who has killed his brother Abel, despairs of God's mercy.
Prologue: Like Cain, Judas despairs of being worthy of mercy and is driven toward the abyss.

Before Caiaphas. Before the members of the High Council enter, Judas considers pleading for his rabbi's life and returning the blood money.

Jesus is being interrogated by Caiaphas in the presence of other members of the Council. He says nothing in response to Caiaphas' questions.
Before the indictment is read, Gamaliel warns the other members of the Council to keep the law and do justice. Jesus is charged with a number of religious violations including blasphemy.
Two witnesses testify to the accuracy of the charges. Jesus does not defend himself.
Gamaliel points out that Jesus is not accused of a crime that is punishable by death or imprisonment.

When asked whether he is the Messiah, Jesus responds in the affirmative.

Gamaliel comes to Jesus' defence, insisting that he considers him a faithful Jew. The others find him guilty of blasphemy, a capital crime. Since only the Romans have the right to order and conduct executions, Jesus will next be taken to the Governor's office.

Judas rushes in and accuses the Council of condemning and murdering an innocent man and pleads for Jesus' life. When he realises that no one listens he curses himself and the members of the Council and plans to commit suicide by hanging himself.

ACT VIII   The First Interrogation by Pilate - Jesus before Herod
            The Second Interrogation by Pilate   -   The Scourging

Tableau: Moses is expelled by the Pharaoh.
Prologue: Like the deluded Pharaoh who refused to let God's people go, Pilate
   refuses to listen to the voice of truth.

Scene 1. - Before Pilate
Members of the Council expect Pilate to support their decision if for no other reason than to gain favour with his appointee, Caiaphas.
Pilate treats the members of the High Council with arrogant disdain, angry at being awakened and their presumption that Caesar's Governor

should serve as blind tool for carrying out their decisions. When told that Jesus called himself the son of God he considers the entire proceeding superstitious nonsense.

Caiaphas then accuses Jesus of being an agitator, a revolutionary.

Pilate admits that he has heard of Jesus, a vagrant, performing magic tricks, but doubts that he is responsible for riots. Caiaphas and the others use Jesus' claim to be the Messiah as proof, since both Jews and Romans understand the term to point to a military leader who will liberate the Jews from the Romans.

Pilate tries to interrogate Jesus who tells him that his kingdom is not of this world. Pilate refuses to authorise the execution, and when he discovers that Jesus comes from Galilee, sends him to Herod, the King of Galilee, who happens to be in Jerusalem for the festival.

Scene 2. - Before Herod
Herod tries to get Jesus to entertain him by causing darkness to fall suddenly or walking without touching the ground or changing a stick into a snake. When Jesus doesn't perform, he calls him a fool who should be let go. Herod has no intention of getting involved in the pious squabbles of the religious leaders, and, after mockingly dressing him in one of his old ceremonial robes, sends Jesus back to Pilate.

Scene 3. - Before Pilate
Caiaphas and Annas do their best to convince Pilate to have Jesus executed. They tell Pilate that they will appeal to the Emperor if Pilate sets Jesus free, and gives him a chance to incite the people to riot, to have him blaspheme the faith, and to have him lead the Jews under the Roman sword.

Pilate agrees to release either Barabbas or Jesus for the Passover festival. Annas and Caiaphas tell some of the other priests to summon their supporters from the streets and do their best to discourage the followers of Jesus from joining the crowd.

Pilate is told of his wife's request to free Jesus, but is more concerned with potentially using Jesus to keep Barabbas, a real revolutionary, from being set free. He orders Jesus flogged by his men.

Facing Page: *Jesus answers his accusers*

Jesus is beaten viciously and collapses. His tormentors dress him in the king's mantle, put the crown of thorns on his head, and hand him a stick for a sceptre. They throw themselves down before Jesus, jeering, "We greet you, great and mighty King of the Jews!"

Musical Selections
The torment is described, repeating the refrain: "See, what a man!"

ACT IX - Jesus, "the King", before the Crowd
Pilate Condemns Jesus to Death

Tableau: Joseph is celebrated as saviour and king of Egypt.
Prologue: In Jesus, the man of sorrows, robbed of all dignity, God's love reveals itself and true majesty is shown. Like once Joseph who saved the starving nation, Jesus saves humanity.

Outrage
Nicodemus tells John that Jesus was condemned to death by the High Council and was then taken before the Governor. Nicodemus still hopes that Pilate won't co-operate. Different groups of people are screaming their support of Barabbas or Jesus. Members of the High Council list the crimes of which Jesus has been accused and urge their followers to clamour for Barabbas to be pardoned. The mob screams that Jesus should pay for his blasphemy on the cross.

In vain, Nicodemus tries to reason with Caiaphas and the others, who accuse him of being followed by prostitutes and tax collectors, and even pagans.

Finally, as Pilate appears, the frenzied mob demands the death of Jesus. Nicodemus and his followers call for setting Jesus free, but they are outnumbered. When Barabbas is brought in, the mob calls for his liberation. When Pilate continues to hesitate, Caiaphas accuses him of not being Caesar's friend and Annas threatens to inform the Emperor that he gave protection to one guilty of high treason. Among screams of "Crucify him," Pilate gives in to their demands. He announces that the death sentence will be prepared in writing and proclaimed in public, and Jesus will be crucified with two murderers.

Facing Page: *He is sentenced*

As the sentence is proclaimed, the crosses are brought. Caiaphas and the other priests rejoice over their victory. The people head for Golgotha – the place of skulls.

ACT X - The Way of the Cross - The Crucifixion

Prologue: Life, compassion, and grace flow for humanity from the cross.
1. Prefiguration: Isaac, Abraham's son carries the wood for his own sacrifice up Mount Moriah. (Gen. 22, 1-13)
2. Prefiguration: Looking at the bronze serpent brings salvation to the Israelites. (4 Mos. 21, 8)

The Way of the Cross
Mary, Lazarus, and Magdalene wonder why the streets are deserted. John tries to keep Mary from going to Golgotha, but she insists, recalling Simeon's prophecy when she brought the infant Jesus to the Temple.

To the hate-filled screams of the mob, driven with sticks, Jesus staggers up the mountain. He stumbles and falls. The guards drag Jesus along. Mary recognises her son. Veronica wipes his face. One of the soldiers forces Simon of Cyrene to carry the cross. A woman asks, "Rabbi, this is how they reward you?" Jesus asks her to weep for herself and her children.

The Crucifixion

Prologue: On the cross, Jesus asks the Father to forgive his enemies, and filled with love, gives up his life, so we will escape eternal death.

When Annas sees the raised cross he is at first delighted, but objects to the inscription,"Jesus the Nazarene, King of the Jews." He demands that it be torn down but is informed that the inscription was attached to the cross by order of the governor and could not be removed.

Members of the High Council and some of the Roman soldiers taunt Jesus. The soldiers throw dice for Jesus clothing. After one of the soldiers mocks him, Jesus asks the Father to forgive them, for they don't know what they are doing. His words apply to both Romans and Jews, as well as all of humanity. When one of the robbers asks for mercy from Jesus he

Facing Page: The Crucifixtion Scene from the 1990 Play

promises that the man will be with him in paradise that very day.
Caiaphas and his followers are appalled at Jesus' arrogance.

Mary and John are approaching the cross. Jesus asks John and Mary to be
each other's support.
A soldier offers a drink to Jesus. After calling to the Father and
commending his spirit to him, Jesus dies.

It begins to thunder. The earth quakes. The sun grows dark. Several
spectators ask Almighty God to have mercy on them. The High Priest is
told that the curtain of the Holy of Holies in the Temple has torn.

When the friends of Jesus hear that the corpses of the dead are to be
thrown into the pit of the criminals, Joseph of Arimathea decides to ask
Pilate for the body of Jesus, so he can be buried in an appropriate
tomb. Nicodemus offers to bring the oils to embalm him.

Mary and Magdalene plead with the soldiers to spare Jesus when they break
the bones of the others. After Jesus' side has been pierced with a
lance, and they are sure he is dead, the soldiers consent.

Members of the High Council are concerned that the disciples of Jesus
could steal the body and then spread the story that he had risen again,
as he had prophesied.

John, Magdalene, and Mary are mourning. Magdalene reminds them of the
words Jesus said when he departed from Bethany, "You will weep and
lament, but the world will rejoice. You will be sad, but your sadness
will be transformed into joy. And no one will be able to take away your joy."

After Nicodemus and the other men have taken Jesus down from the cross
they place his body on Mary's lap. She speaks of him as the light that
came into the world, so that no one who believes in Him might ever perish.

ACT XI – The Resurrection

Prologue
Jesus lives. The anointed one arises and leads humanity toward the
heavenly source of all life.

Appearance of the Risen. The Roman soldiers are tired of keeping watch
at the tomb. The women enter on their way to the tomb. Magdalene says,

how happy she is to be able to pay final honours to her beloved Rabbi. They worry about the heavy stone. Then they notice that the stone has been moved and the tomb is empty. Magdalene enters the tomb where an Angel tells her not to worry, that Jesus has arisen from the dead.

Outside, Jesus speaks to her, but she doesn't recognise him at first. When she does, He asks her to tell the others what has happened. Magdalene rejoices, "I have seen the Lord, I have heard His voice! I know that my saviour lives. . . . Oh, could I proclaim it throughout all the world, that the mountains and rocks and heaven and earth should re-echo with the words:
"Halleluja! He is risen!"

Concluding meditation — musical selection. The Chorus sings a hymn of praise and jubilation.

Notes